MARIE'S TREASURE CHEST

By Marie Simmons
Juliana Whitten Ghostwriter
Present by La Wanda Marrero

TABLE OF CONTENTS
Acknowledgements

ACKNOWLEDGEMENTS

To Julie Whitten

On the behalf of my mother and author, Marie Simmons, THANK YOU for your steadfast commitment in honoring her wish for the completion of her inheritance to her family and friends. This book is an excerpt of her complete memoir *My Life: It's Nothing Personal, and Neither is Yours,* unpublished as yet.

Julie, you are one of her dearest and longstanding, friends who extended over twenty years of help from the beginning of her writing process. You were instrumental in life then and now. I know she is pleased.

Entwined with your dedication is mine—to complete her life's legacy in her absence. Her last spoken words to me were, "Take care of the children and do what's next." In my Aha! moment, I knew that finishing the work on her book was next. I also extend warm gratitude to her church family and friends who have given generously of their time and effort

La Wanda Marrero

THE QUALITIES.

Receiving the wisdom of those who've gone before me, along with the lessons I've learned directly from life, there are a few things I know for sure: *there are universal principles which govern life.* I believe they are the foundation for a meaningful life. The way to ensure that you will receive what you want is to give it. This is the reciprocal nature of the universe, sometimes called the Golden Rule, or Karma; as you do unto others it shall be done to you.

Marie bequeaths her vast "fortune" *--the wisdom of the ages--* to her children, family, friends, and to you, the reader. Your inheritance is to be found in a treasure chest full of precious jewels, named in the upcoming list of Qualities in this golden booklet. Remember, they are not personal! Your personal treasure chest is located in your own backyard. Everybody has one. These Qualities are tools to help you find yours. The universe loves a happy learner. Use your inheritance to guide you in rowing your boat gently down life's stream…merrily! for life is but a dream.

AUTHENTICITY.

"Authenticity is the alignment of head, mouth, heart, and feet - thinking, saying, feeling, and doing the same thing – consistently."
Lance Secretan

"The easiest thing in the world to be is you. The most difficult thing to be is what other people want you to be. Don't let them put you in that position." Leo Buscaglia

In the words of Shakespeare, "To thine own self be true."
"The most common form of despair is not being who you are." Kierkegaard

In the words of Bill Maher, "The privilege of a lifetime is being who you are."

Being authentic empowers self and others. It validates those around us and generates trust, creating a safe and comfortable atmosphere for all. For years I hesitated to speak my truth to avoid hurting others' feelings. I reached a point when it became more painful to repress it than to express it. When I got enough courage to speak out, I noticed that after some initial discomfort and disbelief, even shuffling of the feet, head turning, and eye squinting, people seemed more relaxed and accepting. Self is the only thing any of us really has to share. Know the self.

COMPASSION.

"One love, one heart, one destiny." Bob Marley

"Be kind, for everyone you meet is fighting a harder battle." Plato

When I feel compassion, I am most fully aware of my own humanity and connection with the divine. My first experience at age five of my heart opening was through the door of compassion for children in the orphanage who had no mothers. That moment was pivotal in setting the course for my life, when I made a vow that when I grew up, I would take care of all children without parents.

All major religions emphasize compassion as the primary gateway to heaven. The truth is we are all one, so whatever we do to the Other, we do to ourselves. Love and compassion for others is felt in our own heart.

My mother often repeated the story of a man who felt sorry for himself because he had no shoes, and then he met a man who had no feet. Compassion is a very effective vaccine against feelings of separation, fear, depression, and other negative emotions. One cannot feel compassion and suffer at the same time.

EDUCATION.

" Education is a progressive discovery of our ignorance." Will Durant

"Education is man's going forward from cocksure ignorance to thoughtful uncertainty. Kenneth G. Johnson

"Education is hanging around until you've caught on." Robert Frost

Education is the act of getting something, so you have something to give. Formal education, school, is one door to knowledge. Knowledge is power. My philosophy of education is: "Learn as if you will live forever and live as if you will die tomorrow." I want my epitaph to read: "***She loved, she believed, and she valued education.***" Ironically, we resist the hardest what we need the most. Reflecting on my early strong dislike and resistance to going to school, it's now funny to realize that education has been my saving grace and the key to doors that would have remained locked to me.

As a child, the relevance of reading, writing, and arithmetic to my future well-being totally escaped me. Fortunately, I had a strong mother who knew the many trials and tribulations I would face without it. She said, "My world would be restricted, and I would be doomed to poverty. Just keep breathing in and breathing out, and put one foot ahead of the other, and you will get the hang of it." That was her version of "Fake it til you make it." Going to school was non-negotiable. Of all my accomplishments, receiving a higher education is probably the most important. Being exposed to learning expanded my knowledge and appreciation of life. Because of my education, I believe I am a better person, a better parent, and citizen of the universe; it has not only benefited me, but everyone who knows me. It has expanded my world and made it possible for me to have the financial resources to explore and enjoy it.

Not all education takes place within learning institutions. I believe that the world is a school without walls, and all experiences are lessons designed to help us grow and realize who we really are. Our purpose for being on earth is to shed our illusions of separation and realize our oneness with God, each other, and all there is.

I will always have a deep appreciation for the opportunity to work with dying patients in a hospice program. Death is for me the greatest teacher of life. All the people I worked with who before they died had pre-death experiences told me emphatically that the only question to be asked at the end of life is," How much did you love?"

LOVE.

"Love is an acceptance of all there is, has been, will be, and will not be." Marie Simmons

"Love seeks itself. The more love it finds, the more it gives of itself; the more souls who resonate together, the greater the intensity of their love, for, mirror-like, each soul reflects the others." Dante

"Love is patient, love is kind. It does not envy, it does not boast, it is not proud. It is not rude, it is not self-seeking. It is not easily angered, it keeps no record of wrongs. Love does not delight in evil, but rejoices with the truth. It always protects, always trusts, always hopes, always perseveres. Love never fails." Rumi says,

"The subtle truth is whatever you love you are."

God is love, love is all there is, love is who we are, and love is what we are all looking for. What we are looking for is also looking for us. This has been said many times and in many ways. Love is the pattern that connects us one to the other. As a world citizen and student of the universe, I have learned that we are all alike and we are all different. We can use our similarities to accept and understand our differences. This is affirmed when I see pictures of the human embryonic development from the sperm fertilizing the egg to the birth of the baby. In the beginning of life, there are no beliefs, preferences, fears, or feelings of separation. We are all made from the same dust from distant stars, individual expressions of one Life Force.

Whatever we do to another person we do also to ourselves. It is no small wonder that the Golden Rule is universally recognized--do unto others as you would have them do unto you. In the process of individuation, we are taught or come to believe that we are separate, and sometimes it appears that our well-being is elevated by dominating or being "one up" on others. In truth, dominating another builds walls, creates wars, and prevents connections of the heart. There are no firsts among equals. God dances in relationships between equal partners.

TRUTH.

Gandhi says, "There is no God higher than truth."

The Bible says, "Know the truth and the truth will set you free." (John 8:32)

The Buddhists say, "To realize the inexpressible truth, do not manipulate mind or body, but simply open into transparency with relaxed natural grace."

Hattie Ford says, "A lie can travel around the world but the truth will be right there waiting for it on its return."

The truth simply is--it does nothing and depends on nothing to be itself. It exists with or without awareness, belief, or acceptance. Probably of all the qualities in the world, the practice of truth is the most important to me. Without truth there is no trust, and the heart hides.

A well-loved and highly respected minister told me that he had been lying most of his life. He decided a few years ago to start telling the truth and was absolutely amazed by how free he now feels. His lies included secret affairs, justifying immature behavior like buying cars he didn't need, and denial of his alcoholism. I had bought into his projected image of the evolved man of the cloth. Knowing his foibles endeared him to me. I wondered how many other people were walking around in masks. Then I decided I am one of them...

In the three phases of "The Looking Glass Self," Cooley talks about the way we would like to be seen, the way others see us, and the way we actually are. The discrepancy between the three may lie in the fact that many of us do not allow ourselves to see, know, or share our true selves. In the process of becoming whole, self-examination and discovery are necessary parts of maturing. In the words of Louise Hays, "Whatever you refuse to feel you can't heal." As long as you are in denial, you can't see the problem. When we refuse to feel our feelings, those around us are forced to feel them for us.

We hide from our shadow and project the parts of us that we disown onto others. We try to show others only the parts of us that we want them to see, while our real selves lurk behind our many masks. Our personas of who we would like to be, who we think others expect us to be, become the roles we play in life.

Being willing to look at my own insanity around my smoking addiction opened me to considering that I might be insane in other areas of my life as well. For years I have guided clients through a process of self-exploration and discovery. However, recently when I observed the disarray in my own bathroom, I felt so disgusted that I told myself it was not me. In response another voice asked, "Well, who is it?" In this moment I realized that I disassociate, disown, and do not identify with aspects of my personality or behavior that I do not like. This came as quite a surprise, since I want to see myself as a truth seeker. I remembered my mother quoting Jesus as saying that he came to bring light but man preferred darkness. The discovery of this truth never ceases to amaze me. To varying extents, we all protect ourselves from the cold truth, not realizing we are keeping ourselves in bondage. It's truth, not love, that sets us free!

GENEROSITY.

"There is a wonderful mythical law of nature that the three things we crave most in life -- happiness, freedom, and peace of mind -- are always attained by giving them to someone else." Peyton Conway March

" We make a living by what we get, but we make a life by what we give." Winston Churchill

The evidence of a well-nourished soul is the act of sharing with others. It liberates the soul. I've learned that being generous makes me feel good about myself, when it starts with myself and is extended to others. Starting with an external motivation usually does not end in personal satisfaction. Misguided generosity is worse than hoarding— it can create weakness, resentment on both sides, entitlement, and dependency. True generosity is always based solely on discerning the needs of others.

RITUALS.

"Discipline and practice are the road to the Light. Without them, we plunge back into Darkness." Lao Tzu

Ceremonies and repetitive behaviors are necessary for our social equilibrium and growth. They remind us of our intentions and agreements, and are sources of comfort, reassurance, and joy. All cultures share rituals in some form, especially occasions for celebration: successful plantings and harvests, births, weddings, deaths, rites of passage, etc. All religions have practices to develop one's relationship with the Divine--prayer, meditation, chanting, singing, dancing, baptisms, and initiations. In fact, religion is a verb. It has to be practiced in order to have meaning. Reading about it, talking it, teaching, reflecting, and thinking about it have little benefit without practice.

Likewise, Einstein told us, "Perfection is not an act, or a goal; it is a practice." My soul was stirred when I heard Thich Nhat Hanh's sacred daily meditation. In conversation with the Beloved, he says: "Darling, I am here for you. Darling, I know you are there for me. This awareness makes me very, very happy." Repeating this loving connection is a surefire way of strengthening your connection with God and experiencing joy.

Striving to attain the bliss this monk enjoys, I decided to adapt his meditation to my own life by starting the day with inviting the

Spirit to dress me every morning and opening to follow His direction. Through practicing this ritual, I am perfecting the expression of the Spirit artistically using my body as the canvas. When I become one with this practice, I plan to gradually expand the ritual to include everything I do. Since the beginning of time, we have been advised by our ancestors, "Practice makes perfect."

WORK.

Eric Erikson said, "In order to live a quality life one must love well and work well."

"If you have a task to do, Labor great or small, It's wise to do it well, Or do it not at all." Hattie Ford

"Choose a job you love and you'll never have to work another day in your life." Confucius

"If you are not fortunate enough to choose a job you love, love the job you have." Being busy does not always mean real work. The object of all work is production or accomplishment and to either of these ends there must be forethought, system, planning, intelligence, and honest purpose, as well as perspiration. "Seeming to do is not doing." Thomas A. Edison

I think of my mother and work as almost synonymous. She was always working. Although she was under five feet tall, she was very strong and in constant motion. She was up before the sun, made a large breakfast, got many children off to school, then went to her job at a brickyard, moving bricks in a wheelbarrow. On the weekends she worked cleaning other people's houses, a job I sometimes accompanied her to. Instead of shame I felt pride at seeing my mother being able to take control of large-scale disorder and whittle it down to size. Watching my mother move with such precision and purpose as she worked impressed me greatly. I remember being amazed at a lady's collection of stockings my mother was washing. I am sure this influenced my fascination with fancy stockings, of which I have many.

When my mother was home, she was either cooking or cleaning, and at the end of a day she fell asleep as soon as she sat down to read the paper. She took pride in her work. She didn't take kindly to anyone who avoided work or did a sloppy job. She would call you back to redo it. She always encouraged me to do my best, pointing out that my work was a reflection of me—what I thought about myself, the job, and who I was doing it for. I bitterly complained about having to get up early and promised myself if I ever got grown with a house of my own, I would sleep as long as I wanted; since becoming an adult, however, I automatically wake up at the crack of dawn. 'I still hear my mother's voice saying, "The early bird gets the worm."

I have now discovered that doing a job well not only develops personal competence but also brings deep satisfaction and self-esteem. I worked for many years at my mother's pace, until I realized that I could choose a life of less work and more play. In fact, my mother helped me heal this compulsion toward work by sharing her recurring dream about me being in the kitchen working while others were in the living room having fun. Although work was a dire necessity and a source of great pride for my mother, I also wish her life had been more balanced with fun.

FAITH.

"Fear knocked at the door. Faith answered. And lo, no one was there."
Author unknown

"When we walk to the edge of all the light we have...and take the step into the darkness of the unknown... one of two things will happen. There will be something solid for us to land on...or we will be taught to fly."   Author unknown

"Faith is the bird that feels the light when the dawn is still dark. ..."
Mahatma Gandhi

Faith is the willingness to keep trying, believing that we live in a safe universe and are protected. External reality might not match our internal pictures or even reflect our wishes, but it will always be in our best interest. My mother used to tell me that what's meant for me would know my face, and life would get me to my destination. This was a reflection of her belief in predestination and divine order, which gave me a sense of security. Faith is the substance of things hoped for and the evidence of things unseen. Practices of faith, especially in churches, temples, and other spiritual communities, develop personal courage and strength. Without faith it is impossible to commit to life.

Nita, who was accustomed to making a very large salary, was laid off for a whole year due to the downturn of the economy. This was extremely difficult for her since her bills reflected her customary income. In my efforts to comfort her, I assured her that God was with her and everything would turn out for her highest good. She asked me how I knew. My initial response was to say that I just did, but I remembered that my belief was the result of all my life experiences. Knowing my life had not been a bed of roses, she was comforted by the fact that my life seemed better than ever before. Over time, as we experience the cumulative and unquestionable evidence of God taking care of us, we grow in faith.

I used to think that the definition of insanity was repeating the same dysfunctional behaviors while expecting different results. I now realize that repetitive behavior with awareness is the first step to wisdom; it builds faith, and eventually leads to the Divine. Each time we make a choice to see, hear, and follow God, it builds our relationship with Him and our trust in ourselves. Our faith becomes a little stronger.

COMMITMENT.

"Until one is committed there is always hesitancy,
the chance to draw back, always ineffectiveness.
Concerning all acts of initiative and creation,
there is one elementary truth, the ignorance of which
kills countless ideas and splendid plans:
The moment one definitely commits oneself,
then providence moves too.
All sorts of things occur to help that would never otherwise have
occurred.
A whole stream of events issues from the decision,
raising to one's favor all manner of unforeseen accidents and
meetings and material assistance which no man could have dreamed
would come his way.
Whatever you can do or dream you can, begin it.
Boldness has genius, power and magic in it."   Goethe

I once heard a minister define commitment as a stable thought. According to Tony Robbins, "Life is constantly testing us for our level of commitment, and life's greatest rewards are reserved for those who demonstrate a never-ending commitment to act until they achieve. This level of resolve can move mountains, but it must be constant and consistent. As simplistic as this may sound, it is still the common denominator separating those who live their dreams from those who live in regret."

Commitment is when one makes a choice that says yes to one thing and no to everything else. When one is faced with temptations to betray a commitment, one then has the opportunity to make a conscious choice and to remember that the power within to honor the

Self is stronger than any external force or impulse. This is very challenging to me being a Gemini, who are known for having flighty and contradictory thoughts and ideas. In the past it was not easy for me to hold stable thoughts, which is probably one of the reasons marriage had little appeal for me. The truth is that while I have thought that I was intimidated by commitment, I now realize that my resistance was to being trapped where I didn't want to be.

When I am committed, I am fully committed. For example, faced with the possibility I might have to resign my new job as Chief of the Social Work Department at UCSF when my mother fell, because I was committed to taking care of her there was never a doubt about what I would do. As a result of my strong commitment, the universe provided all manner of support for me to do both. The mystery of surrender brings strength, clarity, expectancy, and faith which remains unchanged regardless of the level of difficulty. It offers a sense of purpose and continuity although the meaning may not be understood. Faith is the reason and result of commitment.

ACCEPTANCE.

"Acceptance is not submission; it is acknowledgement of the facts of a situation . Then deciding what you're going to do about it."
Kathleen Casey Theisen

"Many of us crucify ourselves between two thieves-regret for the past and fear of the future." Fulton Oursler

"Acceptance is integral to commitment. On a committed path we must accept what the journey unveils. Socrates suggested that one should strive for moral clarity rather than moral certainty."

"There is a field beyond right and wrong---meet me there." Rumi

Recently I was faced with the challenge of deciding the mortal fate of my beloved cat Piper. As I walked through the shadow of his death I was robbed by the fear of the financial drain on my future and torn by the deep feelings of love we shared in the past. When I released the past and the future, in the present moment I decided that Piper's spirit was eternal, and my finances required me to be practical and let go of my attachment to his body.

When I told the veterinarian my decision to put him to sleep rather than pay another three thousand dollars for his care, she strongly disagreed and started listing community resources available to me. She began making calls and solicited the help of two pet hospitals plus the Humane Society to work together to assist with the finances to extend Piper's life. Once I accepted the truth of my situation and relaxed into it, the universe moved to support me.

In the past, I have been the provider for others and was more comfortable in this role. Recently I have been forced into the heart opening process of learning to receive gracefully. I now understand why some spiritual paths require seekers to wear tattered clothing and beg for alms—need is the best cure for arrogance and self-importance. I can more freely give others the opportunity to give to me and accept it graciously.

HUMILITY.

"What makes humility so desirable is the marvelous thing it does to us; it creates in us a capacity for the closest possible intimacy with God"
Monica Baldwin

"To be humble to superiors is duty, to equals, courtesy, to inferiors, nobleness." Benjamin Franklin

Humility is freedom from false pride and arrogance; it is the recognition that we are all the same. There are no firsts among equals. The universe is impersonal in its divine laws and perfection. Not knowing what to expect from my own body, and having even less ability to control it, has forced me to live in the mystery rather than the known. It made me become very humble and aware of my own insignificance, helplessness, and mortality. When I get really scared, I drop all defenses and pretenses of having things under control, because it's clear to me that I don't, so I let go, and I let God. And He always comes through.

The truth is that of myself I can do nothing, but the Spirit within can do all things. I am less inclined to increase the burdens of others with my projections and expectations because I realize that we are all doing the best we can with what we have in this Earth School. It is in vulnerability that our safety lies. When we realize we have nothing to lose, we have everything to gain and nothing to defend. When we are humble, we are open, and we can hear the voice of God

FORGIVENESS.

"Unforgiveness is drinking poison hoping someone else will die."
Oprah

"People are often unreasonable, illogical and self-centered; forgive them anyway. You see, in the final analysis, it is between you and God. It was never between you and them anyway." Mother Teresa

Forgiveness is said to be the key to happiness. It is something we do for ourselves, not others. Happiness cannot coexist with resentments. Chronic and lingering anger causes cancer, diabetes, ulcers, high blood pressure, heart disease, and all manner of malaise. Luskin did extensive research at Stanford on the power of forgiveness and published it in his book *Forgive for Good*. It explains how to let go of anger for our own good and the good of others.

Holding on to grievances hurts. It has been said that forgiveness is giving up all hope that the past will be different. When we can stop cursing the past and accept all of our experiences as valuable lessons, it becomes easier for us to thank those who have betrayed us, abused us, lied to us, and mistreated us. They have provided vital opportunities for our growth. When we forgive ourselves for our own imperfections, we are able to look in the mirror and see our divine reflection.

Oprah had a woman on her show who had been very severely burned in a car accident caused by a drunk driver. She shared her process of forgiving him, which was a daily practice to see his innocence, to remember that he did not intend to do her harm. She said that she could only move on with her life after she forgave him.

As much pain and unhappiness that I experienced in my relationship with Melvin, he was the catalyst for my daring move to California which opened a whole new world to me. Richie's beating me woke me up to the reality that Love is the strongest force in the universe and the source of my protection. My emotional and financial betrayal by Faye forced me to look at the devastating consequences of my codependent relationships with my family, and to start the process of setting more healthy boundaries for myself. Most importantly, I forgave myself for my blindness, stupidity, gullibility, vulnerability, the whole ball of wax. It was in my forgiving of my past that I was able to embrace the present and focus on my growth and happiness. I have always been guided by my mother's wisdom and advice. She said, "Never curse the bridge that carries you over."

HAPPINESS.

"On with the dance, let joy be unconfined is my motto, whether there's any dance to dance or any joy to be unconfined." Mark Twain

"wholly to be a fool
while Spring is in the world
my blood approves,
and kisses are a far better fate
than wisdom...." E.E. Cummings

"In the sweetness of friendship let there be laughter, and sharing of pleasures. For in the dew of little things the heart finds its morning and is refreshed." Kahlil Gibran

Play, fun, laughter, joy, pleasure---the spices of life, and the joy of dessert. Laughter and chocolate cake have been known to cure cancer, depression, and other chronic diseases. Happiness lives inside of us and does not depend on external circumstances. Experiencing happiness is *a choice.* We can learn to ride the vicissitudes of life with the same skill as a master surfer riding the Hawaiian waves. Despite the threat of danger and even death, the surfer chooses to enjoy the ride. Some people are afraid to be happy because they anticipate loss. Unfortunately, many people live their lives in quiet desperation and perpetual decay; they are dead before they die. Kindness to ourselves and others is the path to resurrection and new life. Norman Vincent Peale said, "Joy increases as you give it, and diminishes as you try to keep it for yourself."

Life is very short. Appreciate it for the miracle it is, be happy, and share the joy. The happiest people don't necessarily have the best of everything, they just make the best of everything they have.

GRATITUDE.

"The deepest feeling in human nature is the craving to be appreciated." *William James*

"Until we become grateful for what we have, we cannot receive anything new." *Michael Beckwith*

The Course in Miracles states that God is not far from a grateful heart. My church proclaimed "Living in Gratefulness" as its focus for last year. This theme implies that when one is grateful, the practice of gratitude also makes one great. Gratitude not only elevates one's consciousness and changes feeling states, it also invites the universe to give us more of what we are grateful for. As I have felt more dependent over the past ten years, I have become increasingly grateful for the help that I have received from family and friends. When people feel appreciated, they seem to delight in doing for others because it gives them a feeling of purpose and importance.

I have included in my spiritual practice creative ways of expressing the art of thank you. Failure to acknowledge kindness in some form of thanks is equivalent to giving the finger to another's generosity. When I realized this truth, I became ashamed of the many times I have accepted kind deeds but didn't take the time to express my appreciation. Not properly acknowledging the giver minimizes our experience of receiving. When you drink water, remember who dug the well.

In the past, I have been more identified with the giver, and there is a part of me that still prefers that role because it is the symbol of strength in our society, while receiving is more often associated with weakness. The giver is twice blessed: it's a blessing to be able to give, and to be received.

On a recent trip across the Golden Gate Bridge, I commented to a friend that I am in awe every time I cross a bridge. My mind is not mechanical and it absolutely amazes me how a bridge could be built over water. I am also humbled every time I look out of my windows at the magnificent combination of water, trees, mountains, and sky. No matter how often I look at it, it is never the same. My friend said that I was very lucky because once he has seen something, it loses interest for him. I felt compassion for him knowing that his life is greatly diminished by the absence of gratitude. Parents, teach your children the art of please and thank you, or they will be handicapped in life.

ACKNOWLEDGEMENT.

"All beings long for recognition and acknowledgement: do you see me? Do you hear me? Does what I have to say mean anything to you?" Oprah

Acknowledgement is the recognition of the presence of another. I remember with deep affection the greeting given by my spiritual teacher Baba. "I welcome you all with great love with all my heart." Recognizing and greeting each other in our daily lives is a way of vali-dating the importance of our existence. When a greeting is done with love, it has the power to affirm and elevate. Even animals recognize each other and their owners with greetings. A smile, a nod, a friendly word are universal means of connecting with others.

Once a roommate expressed his appreciation of my appearance with such a delightful and sincere acknowledgement, it brightened my entire day. As I was going up the steps, he commented, "Looking gooooood today!" I had provided him with a pleasurable experience which he acknowledged. It is my desire to pass on to the next generation the importance of acknowledging each other. As we all know, a few hellos, goodbyes, pleases and thank yous go a long way.

Our self-image and identity are formed by what other people reflect to us about who or what they think they see in us. I make a point of greeting my foster sons every morning and evening and wishing them well when-ever we depart. I always acknowledge their presence when they enter a room. In this way I affirm their importance to me. The truth is that people like people who like them. Those who are not acknowledged, agreed with, or affirmed feel invisible and unimportant. In this way it is exceedingly difficult if not impossible to feel good enough about oneself to believe that one deserves the gifts of the universe. Every child wants to be the one who lights up his or her mother's face.

PATIENCE.

"God sends us children to teach us patience." Mary Howitt

"Patience is the ability to idle your motor when you feel like stripping your gears." Michael LeFan

Having accepted the reality that I have little or no control over my life, I am learning to accept what is and to be patient about waiting on what's to come. I no longer experience intense anxiety, which was customary for me whenever I asked for or wanted something I did not have. I felt that if it didn't appear immediately, it probably would not. I used to feel reassured only by seeing concrete evidence. I now rest easy when evidence is unseen. When outcomes are requested in the Spirit, I am much more patient and assured of the expected arrival. As I have grown in understanding, I have made peace with Divine Timing.

A friend told me a true story about a woman who said she wanted more patience. He described her as weaving in and out of traffic, swearing at other drivers, making sudden and unexpected stops, and swerving at high speeds. He reminded her that she had asked for more patience and she responded, "Not now! I'm in a hurry!" This story ignited primal laughter in me, and I still laugh whenever I think about it because I realize this is exactly what I did! In the words of St. Augustine, "The reward of patience is patience."

SACRIFICE.

"One-half of knowing what you want is knowing what you must give up before you get it." Sidney Howard

"He who never sacrificed a present to a future good or a personal to a general one can speak of happiness only as the blind do of colors." Olympia Brown

"In this world it is not what we take up, but what we give up, that makes us rich." Henry Ward Beecher

According to the teaching of Jesus, there is no greater love than the love of a man who lays down his life for a friend. Jesus also said, "We have to give up our self to find our self," and he set the ultimate dramatic example of giving up his life (ego) so that man could have life and have it more abundantly. Most mothers and fathers willingly sacrifice or give up self-centered desires in the service of their children. Freud talks about sacrifice as delaying immediate gratification for a future more rewarding goal. He refers to this as "the reality principle."

The important thing is: To be willing at any moment to sacrifice what we are for what we could become. When we are able to get the small self out of the way, the power of the spirit, the strongest force in the universe, is allowed to flow through unobstructed. Self-sacrifice is the real miracle out of which all other miracles grow. The universal law is that those who are not willing to sacrifice will be sacrificed.

RESPONSIBILITY.

"We all have dreams. But in order to make dreams into reality, it takes an awful lot of determination, dedication, self-discipline, and effort." Jesse Owens

"Within each of us lies the power of our consent to health and sickness, to riches and poverty, to freedom and to slavery. It is we who control these, and not another." Richard Bach

Responsibility is owning our responses to all situations, things, and people, and accepting the consequences of our choices. This means being fully present in the moment of now; in this way we identify with the witness consciousness and can see what we are doing. We are then free to change behaviors that are not working for us.

Integrity is the foundation for this work. If integrity were cheap, everybody would have it. In my experience when we are willing to take responsibility for our own actions, it is not only empowering, it's also directive. Then the laws of the universe will show us what we need to do to succeed. We are conditioned to be responsible or not depending on our family, our peers, and our society. The examples and expectations of those we love determine our attitudes about responsibility.

On subtle levels, we are programmed as young children to avoid taking responsibility when we are punished or ridiculed for undesirable behaviors. Because we want to please, we resist being wrong or accepting blame, so we learn to project the cause of our pain outside of ourselves. When children are taught that they can control their behavior and impact outcomes, they are encouraged to take personal responsibility for their lives. When I take responsibility for my behavior, it makes the other person feel more secure, safe, and comfortable in relating to me. It also encourages the other to do likewise.

I have had a habit of leaving my shoes at the top of the steps before going into the carpeted area in my house. My roommates, not expecting the shoes to be there, have tripped over them several times and called my attention to the fact. Old habits are hard to break, and recently I forgot and left my shoes there again. I apologized to one of my roommates and he started making excuses for me, saying he really didn't mind. Initially, I started to engage in a conversation with him about his tolerance, but soon realized that it was more about me than him. I told him in a very resolved tone of voice that it was my responsibility to put my shoes in the appropriate place. A look of relief and serenity showed in his face. I am sure that everyone is relieved when we are willing to take full responsibility for our actions, with no need to involve anyone else.

The pattern of avoiding responsibility is often prevalent in romantic relationships because in the dynamic emotional interaction and merging of two people in love, it's sometimes hard to discern who is responsible for what. It is easy to blame and find fault with the other because it allows us to maintain an idealized self-image and blinds us to our need to change. The pitfall of external blaming is that it is an escape into victimhood and keeps us stuck in the problem. "When we refuse to feel our own feelings, someone else has to." For example, children often take on unexpressed feelings of their parents. When passive aggressive people deny their feelings and act them out, the pain and anger is felt by others.

Although we might be powerless to change external situations, the way we respond to them is up to us. The only person we can change is ourselves. Therefore, it is important to know what self-changes are necessary for the desired result. The truth is that we are 100% responsible for whatever happens to us in any relationship. Choosing to act rather than react is the mature response in any situation.

As I move into deeper levels of self-awareness, I have discovered behaviors and attitudes of mine which are unacceptable to my ego. I understand in a new way why it has been labeled "the shadow" we repress and disown aspects of ourselves that are unflattering, yet they linger in the background, controlling from afar. I have become aware of my tendency to abdicate personal responsibility when it was inconvenient. I have allowed someone else to make choices for me and then became annoyed and felt betrayed when they did not make the "right" one, that is, the choice I thought I would have made, if I had been paying attention and been willing.

I have also observed my tendency to express my feelings rather than choose an effective response to a situation. For example, I was working on a project with an engineer and an architect, both of whom were difficult for me. They talked fast, with thick accents and defensive macho attitudes. I found them very annoying. I knew that expressing anger or casting blame would not facilitate communication, yet I was very tempted to let them know what I thought about their arrogant and self-serving motivations. I did this on two occasions, getting myself into a verbal tug of war that I was not prepared for. The ineffectiveness of these interactions inspired me to hold my ego (tongue and emotions) in check, and to call on patience to allow right action or inaction to flow through me.

Taking full responsibility is the only sure way to get where you want to go in life. Sometimes we interpret failure as meaning something is wrong with us. The truth is when our behavior does not bring the desired results, it is not a statement about who we are but about what we are doing. One can become very frustrated and discouraged trying to fit a square peg in a round hole.

I am aware that I still have impulses to blame, make wrong, and punish others. The experience of having to evict my niece was very painful and I felt victimized for weeks, angry that she "put me in this position after all I had done for her." The more helpless I felt, the angrier I became. I was shocked into facing reality when, upon hearing she was to be evicted, she told another niece that I would just have to do what I had to do. This sounded very simple, and it was clearly the solution to the problem.

However, because I did not want to be the bad guy and evict

her, I had been unwilling to solve the problem that had distressed me for many months. I do not like seeing my character defects, yet they are still a part of me, and I have to "feel it to heal it." I pray that my self-defeating behavior will soon become unattractive even to me. I am renewing my commitment to behave in ways that serve the good of all and the harm of none.

TRUST.

"Trust placed anywhere other than the self is misplaced."
Marie Simmons

Trust is the belief that the best is yet to come. It is the sense that something more powerful than yourself is governing the universe and protecting you. Trust takes practice, and eventually leads to faith. It is first established between an infant and a caregiver. Through availability, responsiveness, and consistency, the caregiver earns the baby's trust, and the baby comes to trust the caregiver's reliability. From this foundation trust can grow, as a flower in fertile soil. Without trust, the child sees the universe as a dangerous place and develops defenses which separate and prevent him or her from experiencing love. These children often become neurotic, psychotic, even sociopaths-- people without the ability to care for or empathize with others.

Without trust, we become control freaks and hold tenaciously to the past. The fear of moving outside of the known confines us to resisting all things new. It's important to understand the past to avoid the experiences you don't want to repeat. However, being attached to or controlled by past memories which are only seen through personally tinted lenses is life draining.

SURRENDER.

"Change is the essence of life. Be willing to surrender what you are for what you could become." Mirela

"Spontaneity is discovered not through action but through refraining from one's habitual actions and seeing what happens next." Author unknown

"The creative process is a process of surrender, not control." Julia Cameron

For years I have prayed for the ability to discern the difference between surrender and resignation. I concluded that resignation is the reluctant attitude of "I have to do this," while surrender is the loving offering of the personal will: "This is mine to do." Opening to receive spontaneity I give up rigidity, and I willingly exchange the false security of the cocoon with freedom. Freedom is our birthright from which all other gifts flow--we are always free to choose our thoughts and actions. Since all feelings are the results of our thoughts, when we change our thinking, we change our world.

I believe that the only thing that separates us from our highest potential and desire is our mind. Our ego wants to be right, to be first, to be better, more than...etc. It is hard to accept that our past experiences, beliefs, and attitudes create our current realities especially when we don't like the external manifestations. We are quite willing to take responsibility for inviting the things we want into our lives! Giving up control is a very abstract construct because we understand and act with the same mind which decides when we've achieved it. Because we want to retain our position, we often delude ourselves into thinking that we are surrendered. Subsequently we are bewildered and confused by undesirable outcomes. The universe conspires to manifest our beliefs, attitudes, and intentions, even when we insist otherwise. We resist the truth that we are co-creators with the universe because it is so difficult to acknowledge and accept that we are in our own way. We cling to the idea that our mis-creations are caused by something or someone outside of ourselves.

One of my most important lessons in surrender came when I was working as a social worker for Children's Services. A co-worker and I were working on a Saturday when the office was usually closed. A deranged father got into the building, pulled a gun on the two of us, demanding to see his children who were not there but in foster homes. We were both terrified. At first, I felt powerless and helpless. Then I remembered my Sunday School lesson that God is all powerful. Accepting this truth, I rose above my fear and started to reason with the man. He slowly calmed down as I talked to him, and he put the gun away. I surrendered to love, and it protected us.

The second experience was when I was beaten up by a six-belt karate champion, who I knew had the capacity to kill me, and probably would have, if I had not risen above my fear. When my consciousness changed to love, his blows somehow ricocheted and returned to him. He soon became exhausted and went to bed. When he was sound asleep, I got out of there. One thing I know for sure is that at the end of fear is love.

CREATIVITY.

"I am certain of nothing but the holiness of the heart's affections and the truth of imagination." John Keats

"The creative is the place where no one else has ever been. You have to leave the city of your comfort and go into the wilderness of your intuition. What you'll discover will be wonderful. What you'll discover is yourself." Alan Alda

We are co-creators with God. Our purpose for being here is to create. Our creations are reflections of our thoughts, attitudes, and beliefs. It is done unto us as we believe. The universe only says yes. Everything we do or fail to do are our creations. We are the instrument through which God is expressed.

Creativity has been the most stabilizing force in my life. It is the external validation of the Spirit within me. All of my creative projects have woven the tapestry of my life. A short list would include raising five girls and many other children and adults; also, development of the cabin, the Center, the CARE Program for UC, an inter-generational family quilt project, my home and its many transitions, writings, my therapy practice, my foster care, my extensive collection of Shona sculpture, and all of the things I failed to do. My personal presentation in the world reflects my deep appreciation of art and color, shapes and designs. Interior decorating and feng shui intuition are two of my most cherished gifts. I've been blessed with the gift to connect with others through my heartfelt prayers. My life story has been expressed in my creativity. Greatness comes from offering our unique gifts to others. "Not everybody can be famous, but everybody can be great." Dr. Martin Luther King

SOLITUDE.

"If you're lonely when you're alone, you're in bad company."
Marie Simmons

"Loneliness is the poverty of the self; solitude is the richness of the self." May Sarton

"I never found the companion that was so companionable as solitude."
Thoreau

Most of my life I have been a very social person who enjoyed being with other people. I hosted and attended many parties, was frequently surrounded by friends and family, including groups of children and animals. Uncharacteristically, for many years I have spent most of my time alone deeply consumed by "the process." During this time, I considered external demands for my attention to be distractions. I quickly became impatient with telephone calls which extended beyond five minutes and could hardly wait to return to my obsession, which had become my form of meditation. It often lasted as long as fifteen hours or more! I remember hearing a story about a meditator complaining to his teacher about people walking over his feet during meditation practice. His teacher said that if he were truly focusing on his meditation, he would not have been bothered by the person walking over his feet. At the time I wondered how it was possible for one to be so deep in meditation and now I know. I felt that I was still in the world but not of it.

With this experience I have become equally comfortable in the worlds of solitude or social settings, but my preference leans towards being with my Self. I know with new certainty that it is not the world that sustains me; it does not define who I am, nor does it determine my worth or well-being. I have re-entered the world with gusto by becoming a foster parent. Once again, I am surrounded by people, activities, noise, and external demands; however, I am practicing being centered in myself while in the eye of the storm and listening to the quiet voice within. Guided by this voice, I am amazed at my increasingly calm acceptance of what is. I am less burdened with *the illusion* of my responsibility for changing anyone or anything. I have found solitude to be my road to peace.

ABOUT THE AUTHOR

Marie Simmons was born in 1936 in St. Louis, Missouri, where her African American family struggled with many of the problems resulting from racism, poverty, and inadequate education. Marie is the youngest of thirteen children and the first in her family to graduate from college. She earned a Master's Degree in social work from Washington University. She has held a variety of professional positions, including the Director of Social Services at UCSF for twelve years, where she was also an assistant professor in the Department of Pediatrics. During a two-year sabbatical from her directorship, she developed and facilitated a Cultural Awareness and Race Relations Education program for the UCSF campus: faculty, staff, and students. She has more than forty years' experience working as a psychotherapist, family counselor, administrator, consultant, teacher, and researcher. She has written a number of professional papers and lectures.

Ms. Simmons was married briefly, and raised many children for many years. She assisted many adult children to grow up by teaching them the art of gentle self-discipline.

She was raised Baptist but always believed that the Spirit is universal. She has been a seeker all of her life and has studied many religions ranging from Christianity to Hinduism to Buddhism and everything in between. She was surprised to discover that in truth all these disciplines are saying the same thing: We are all one, and we should love one another as Ourself. She is convinced beyond any doubt that there are many roads to the mountain, but only one top, and the top is Love. She asked God to teach her to love indiscriminately and unconditionally. The first lesson love taught her was that it is not personal. For the past ten years she has been involved in an intense physical and mental experience of a spiritual transformation which has led to the writing of this book.

www.ingramcontent.com/pod-product-compliance
Lightning Source LLC
Chambersburg PA
CBHW030731150426
42813CB00051B/419